Joanie's Design Elements

8 Easy Lessons to Adapt and Use Quilting Designs

Joanie Zeier Poole

©2007 Joanie Zeier Poole

Published by

krause publications
An Imprint of F+W Publications

700 East State Street • Iola, WI 54990-0001
715-445-2214 • 888-457-2873
www.krausebooks.com

Our toll-free number to place an order or obtain a free catalog is (800) 258-0929.

The following registered trademark terms and companies appear in this book: Supreme Slider™, Canson®, Teflon®, and Golden Threads.

Library of Congress Control Number: 2007922991

ISBN 13: 978-0-89689-522-5
ISBN 10: 0-89689-522-X

Designed by Donna Mummery and Heidi Bittner-Zastrow
Edited by Barbara Sunderlage
Illustrated by Joanie Zeier Poole

Printed in China

Acknowledgments

Nothing in my life would be possible if not for the gifts I possess from Heaven above. I am ever grateful for and thoroughly enjoy the artistic abilities that enrich my life with simple pleasures. I cherish the experience of creating each quilt, from choosing the fabrics and threads, to designing a canvas filled with unique images. I understand that any talent is precious and was intended to be utilized. I gain purpose in my life by sharing my ideas that relieve your perceived artistic limitations in completing your own quilts. As my world expands with the opportunities these abilities provide me, so do the blessings I receive from you, my students returning even more gifts back into my life.

I also want to acknowledge that my world is rich with a supportive husband, two self-reliant sons, a loving family and faithful friends. And I wish to thank everyone at Krause who added their skills to the existence of this book, especially Susan, Candy, Heidi and Bob. Thanks for your encouragement, knowledge and patience.

Contents

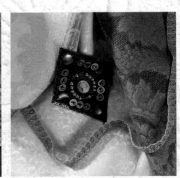

Eight Easy Lessons to Adapt and Use Quilting Designs

INTRODUCTION

Why I Teach

You might say I bring an unconventional approach to quilting. Sure, I have been quilting all of my adult life, but it's the experiences I've had outside the quilt world that has lead me to write this book. I bring a lifelong pursuit of art education, twenty years' experience of hanging wallpaper, my self-taught method for painting large children's murals, and a recent degree in computer graphics. I have combined my creative abilities with my passion for quilting and developed my own method for filling empty quilt tops with original, perfectly-fitting designs.

When I teach design classes, students arrive with the same questions:

"How do I finish my quilt tops?"

"How do I know what designs to put where?"

"How do I get designs to fit the spaces?"

I no longer struggle with doubt when I create a new quilt because through years of practice, I have gained confidence in my artistic choices and you will too, as you work through the lessons of this book.

The joy I experience from transforming a patchwork canvas into a sculptured, dimensional quilt is a satisfaction I could never release to someone else. My quilts begin with a well-developed plan that includes the quilting designs with the patchwork or appliqué in the layout. Since I have always quilted my own quilts, I don't separate the assembly of the top and completion of the quilting into two separate tasks.

I acknowledge that having the ability to visualize a successful design is a gift. I see inspiration for quilts everywhere I look and have trained myself to study the lines of complicated images and interpret them into stitchable designs. I treasure the passion that overtakes me when I am creating my quilts, driving me to develop a construction process to achieve a certain look I desire when no process currently exists. Over the years, I have worked diligently to refine the skills needed to turn my dreams into reality. I gained assurance for decision-making, from practice, and from an acceptance that these abilities truly are blessings. Now, having watched light bulbs spark in the minds of my students, I realize my purpose is to share these gifts with you.

Dear R... unconventional
You might ... ve been
approach to quilting. ... ut it was
quilting all of my adult life ... outside
the impact of what I have done outside
the quilt world that has l... to
write this book.

Words of Motivation

My intent for writing this book is to motivate you through knowledge. You may lack confidence in your own artistic abilities. No need to worry. The lessons within this book will provide you with a foundation for making creative decisions. As with any endeavor in life, not knowing how to proceed can hold you back, so knowledge can be very empowering. This book is filled with imaginative ideas and eight easy lessons that demonstrate a simple and logical approach to the quilting process. The enclosed CD is full of beautiful designs to stimulate you to finish your own quilt tops. These instructions are adaptable to quilters of all skill levels and all methods of quilting. We begin the process by building your decision-making confidence. You will learn how to develop a list of images that enhance your quilt and you'll learn where to find them. Next, you will make paper templates for each area that needs quilting and find many ways to divide those spaces. Learn how adaptable a single stencil can be, removing any restrictions to using it only as the manufacturer expected. From merely changing the size of a design, to isolating portions to be used on their own, to adding your inspiration, you will be in charge of making any motif fit your needs.

In this world of cake mix quilts, I offer you the chance to create your own delicious icing. I don't consider this a derogatory term. On the contrary, boxed cake mixes are a wonderful foundation for whatever embellishments you add, but make it your own! Many quilting books and patterns are available with recipes for wonderful quilt tops, but they are someone else's vision left empty for you to complete. Using these lessons, you will expand your imagination and make quilts that are uniquely your own.

It is with great joy and excitement that I bring this information to you. May it provide you with a firm foundation on which to build your confidence, elevate your expectations, and believe in what you can achieve. Remember, "When we experience joy in what we create, we have found our purpose in life."

Joanie

How to Use This Book

This book is written from the teacher's perspective while teaching a class. The students ask questions, the answers are demonstrated in the lessons. First, read the entire book. Assemble the suggested supplies to make the project easy and enjoyable. Next, learn how to look for and create simple quilting designs. Then try the exercise project. Make the templates and divide the spaces. Follow the simple instructions for sizing the designs to fit. Absorb the tips for marking and for quilting with a home sewing machine.

How to Use the CD

I have included several of my original designs on the CD you'll find in the back of this book. Like any copyrighted material, they are for your personal use only and are not to be used for commercial purposes, nor copied for gifting, sharing or sales.

When you insert the CD-ROM into your computer, the menu may not appear on your screen automatically. To view the CD-ROM menu, click on the Start button on the lower left corner of your screen. Select My Computer. Then double click on Joanie's Design CD.

On the CD-ROM you will find 31 PDF files. Double click a PDF file to view the quilt design. Most computers will display the individual quilt design immediately when you double click it. If your computer will not display the quilt designs, you may need to download a free computer program called Adobe Reader. Adobe Reader is available for download at www.adobe.com.

Note to Teachers and Designers

If you are considering teaching from this book, you must be willing to adhere to all copyright laws. Credit must be given to the author for the intellectual property of the concept, process and designs contained in the text and on the CD. Since copyright law prohibits copying any part of the book or CD for any commercial use, teaching from the text is allowed only when each student in the class is required to purchase an individual copy of the book.

Anyone who designs patterns and would like to suggest that this process aids in completing the quilt, should recommend the purchase of the book. The law also prohibits reprinting or rewording of these intellectual concepts in patterns designed by anyone other than the author.

Necessities, Supplies and Tools You'll Need

Having everything you need on hand before you begin makes any job go more smoothly. Here is a list of equipment and supplies used for the lessons in this book. These tools will help you discover, resize, adapt, mark and stitch designs. Assemble a few basic sewing and art supplies and then follow my suggestions for making our task quicker and easier using modern technology. This is quilting in the new millennium.

Paper

Since when do we need so much paper to quilt? I use inexpensive paper to create layouts, copy motifs and make templates. I draw on it, cut it and stitch through it. Here are several kinds of paper that you'll find useful.

- **Craft Paper**—used for the templates and can be found at craft stores in 12" x 18" sheets and in long rolls sold as shelf liner or art paper for children.

- **Graph Paper**—used for designing and drawing layouts to scale.

- **Canson® Tracing Paper**—my favorite brand of tracing paper. It's sturdy enough to slide through a printer and then stitch through.
  If you don't have a copy machine, use it for tracing multiple copies of motifs for auditioning.

- **Golden Threads Quilting Paper**—trace and stitch designs right through the paper.

- **Freezer Paper**—can be used instead of craft paper. It is readily available in long rolls, is somewhat translucent for tracing, and can be lightly pressed to temporarily fuse to fabric.

Computers and Copy Machines

Computers are becoming increasingly integrated into our quilting processes. They can make life much easier with access to the Internet as well as design software. Many tasks in the following lessons require several copies of a design. Copy machines or a computer with a scanner and printer can be used equally well for this purpose. Your decision about which of these to use may be as simple as which equipment you have access to. The copy machine may have the advantage of using larger paper, yet it may be limited to preset sizes for enlargements and reductions.

Keep your eye out for a copy machine that has specific settings and can increase to 400%. If you are limited to a machine with preset percentages, choose the setting that is smaller than the area to be filled. It is easier to fill in space around a design that is too small than to use a design that is too large. When you are at the copy center, ask to use their proportional scale. They usually have one hidden away behind the counter.

> ### tip:
> Most printers for home computers will print on legal size (8½" x 14") paper. Those extra few inches may give that little added design space you need.

With a copy machine or computer, scanner and printer you can:

- Change the size of a design
- Cut out portions of the design to develop alternate designs
- Create border designs for layout of mitered corners
- Print full-size designs from books (like *Elegant Machine Quilting* from Krause Publications)
- Enlarge magazine images to create drawings
- Audition full-size templates for quilting designs
- Print out the quilting design (to stitch through) on tracing paper

With a computer, scanner and printer you can:

- Print out words, initials, or quotes to be used for stitching guides
- Find clip art and print out ideas for quilting designs, emblems and thread illustrations

Artist's Tools and Art Supplies

Purchase these basics at quilt shops, art supply centers and university bookstores if you don't already have them on hand.

- Mechanical pencil and eraser
- Scissors for cutting paper
- Masking and clear tape
- Quilter's Assistant Proportional Scale by Golden Threads. This handy tool calculates the percentages needed for resizing designs.

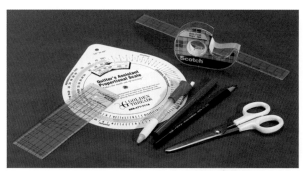

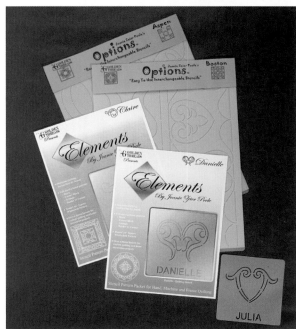

These quilting stencils I designed offer many options for filling the various areas of the quilt top. They are available through GoldenThreads.com

Pens and Pencils

There are too many brands and styles of marking tools to mention. I keep my choice simple and rely on what gives the best results. If you have prewashed your fabric you need not worry about removing markings with cold water. Be sure to test each fabric with the marker you intend to use to be sure you can remove it completely.

- Quilting stencils are commercially-made plastic sheets with a wide variety of cut out quilting designs.
- Wash-away markers are available in blue for marking most fabrics. Marking pencils are available in light colors for marking dark fabric.
- Clover now makes an eraser pen to remove any mistakes made with the wash-away marker. If a mistake is made, correct it with the blue marker first, then remove any unwanted lines.
- A light box enables you to see design lines through dark fabrics. It may also be useful in the design phase of this process. You can make your own by inverting a plastic storage bin and placing a light strip inside.

Thread

For refined free-motion work, the scale of the designs and background fillers are reduced. The use of very lightweight thread (100-weight silk by YLI and 60-weight 2-ply polyester by Superior Threads) allows the quilting design itself to be highlighted rather than the thread. Invisible thread can also be used in the top of a machine with lightweight thread in the bobbin. The needle size must be adjusted to the size and style of the thread. For 60-weight thread, use a #70 or #80 needle. For 100-weight or invisible thread, use a #60 or #70 needle.

For this style of quilting, thread is matched to the color of the fabric and used to outline the designs. It's necessary that the selection of other supplies enhance visual dimension, causing quilting designs to visually pop off the quilt surface.

- The sheen of cotton sateen fabric reflects light to highlight quilting designs.

- Hobb's Heirloom or Tuscany Wool Battings are made of soft natural fibers that compress easily to fit under the machine head and flatten for background fillers, yet are lofty enough to fill puffy shapes. Since I have been using this batting, trapunto has not been necessary. It is lightweight, therefore reducing stress on back muscles when maneuvering a large quilt.

Workspace Setup

Set up a comfortable workspace for machine quilting to avoid aches and pains. Provide adequate lighting and an adjustable chair.

- If you are far-sighted like I am, you will reduce eye strain by using a magnifying light. Proper lighting is vital when you are working on intricate designs.

- The Supreme Slider is a Teflon sheet with a self-stick backing that attaches to the bed of a sewing machine. Your quilt sandwich will glide as you free motion machine quilt.

- Use an adjustable-height office chair that has good back support.

You know the saying about having the right tool for the job. Honor your time and effort by using the best tools and materials that you can afford in each step of the process. You are worth it. And remember to enjoy what you are creating. This is the fun part of our lives!

Sewing Machine

Achieving great results with heirloom machine quilting does not require a fancy sewing machine, although manufacturers are continually adding wonderful features to their machines. The quilter's skill and practice are as important as a clean, well-maintained machine. Establish a relationship with a dealer in your area who can provide information on the specifics of your machine. With any free-motion quilting, the feed dogs are lowered and a darning foot is attached.

Learning the technique of free-motion quilting has changed my quilting world. Using this skill, I have created artwork for this book as well as to exhibit at quilt shows. I'm astonished by comments from viewers who really have no idea that it's even possible to quilt full-size quilts on a home sewing machine. My mission in life is to inform quilters that this is an attainable skill and to provide them with information to quilt with a home sewing machine. I also want to entice them to learn while creating beautiful projects. For more information on supplies and preparation for heirloom machine quilting, refer to my first book, *Elegant Machine Quilting*. For a look at my award-winning quilts, visit my Web site www.heirloomquiltingdesigns.com.

Glossary of Frequently Used Terms

- Block—a square section of the quilt top; could be appliqué, patchwork or plain fabric
- Border—strips of fabric used to frame the center layout of a quilt
- Centerline—a line that marks the crosswise center of a border
- Corner block—a square quilting design set in the corners of the borders
- Cornerline—the 45-degree diagonal line that divides the intersection of two borders
- Filler object—a small quilted shape used to fill empty space
- Fill patterns—repeated patterns that are used to fill background space
- Free-motion quilting—stitching lines using a sewing machine with a darning foot and feed dogs lowered
- Focus fabric—medium- to large-scale print fabric that dictates the color choices
- Grids—straight lines stitched in patterns forming squares or diamonds
- Layout—the quilt composition; planned placement for the blocks and borders
- Motif—one individual quilting design
- Segments—equal portions of a template
- Setting triangles—triangular pieces of fabric used to fill the side and corner spaces created when blocks are set on point
- Stencil—a thin sheet of plastic with cut-out designs used for tracing quilting designs
- "Stitchable design"—a phrase I coined for outlines of images that are simple enough to stitch with a line of stitching
- Stippling—a curving, continual line of stitching that densely fills the background of a quilt top and the space around quilted motifs
- Template—in this book, refers to a piece of paper cut to the exact size and shape of the empty space on a quilt that needs to be filled with quilting designs

Lesson One:

Finding *Your* Design Style

In Lesson One, you will learn how to:

- Find your own personal style
- Develop a theme for your project (if you want a theme)

Getting Started

You'll begin with recognizing what you like, and that simple understanding will build your confidence in making choices. Soon you'll realize that you really do have a distinct personal style and you've been making design decisions your entire life.

How do I choose the right quilting designs for each quilt?

To tell you there is an exact formula for choosing the perfect quilting design for every quilt would be like saying there is only one correct piece of jewelry to complement an outfit. We all know there are many choices for very interesting embellishments. The fun comes in experimenting with many options to find your favorite. Everyone has personal panache; his or her own unique taste. Thank goodness! Wouldn't it be boring if we couldn't decide how to make our little corner of the world unique?

Getting back to the question, how much help would I be in guiding your quilting decisions to just repeat the same old generalizations you've heard before? It's true that curving lines of quilting do contrast with geometric patchwork, and that using diagonal grids to fill the background around appliqué might be good advice for a reproduction piece. But that doesn't provide you with helpful information to create quilts that show your personal flair. You need to learn what possibilities are available, and where to find designs that really add beauty to your particular quilt.

How do I find inspiration that reflects my unique style?

This quilt was inspired by the design of an antique brooch

We each have our own personal style. You just might not have the confidence to realize it yet. Or, you may be living under the misconception that either you have it, or you don't and never will. I believe it can be developed, nurtured and enjoyed.

Develop your power of observation. Your style is reflected in the choices you make. Look around your home at objects of art and decoration. Study items of beauty you take pleasure in, the design of your furniture and the fabrics you have chosen. Peruse the pages of your favorite magazines. Do they reflect the style of your home?

Browse your bookshelves and those at your local library for examples of artistic expression that you find attractive. Look for objects that are sculpted, having depth on their surfaces like wood and stone carvings. Books about jewelry, patterned glass, old postcards, labels, and architectural details offer inspiration. Take a moment to imagine how the shapes could be used as quilting designs. Recently, I have found inspiration from old Victorian decorating magazines. They have provided a treasure trove of elegant quilting design ideas for my latest quilts.

If a pattern catches your eye, make a scan or photocopy of it. Save these ideas in an idea notebook organized in categories to be used as an inspirational resource. If you lack the confidence to recognize your own style, this compilation will help you identify where you find beauty. This system works for choosing clothing or home décor, so rely on it when choosing quilting designs. Heighten your awareness of design in your everyday environment and prepare to be inspired!

How do I develop ideas for a quilt?

When you begin a new quilt, consider your intent. Will it be elegant, whimsical, or masculine? Choose a theme and stick with it when choosing the fabric, the pattern and the quilting designs. Designing the entire piece, from assembly through quilting, is much easier if you limit your choices to one basic category.

For instance, if you intend to use reproduction 1930s fabrics, let your fabrics direct the design decisions. Look for a patchwork or appliqué pattern from that era. With a little research, you will find many examples displaying appropriate quilting designs.

If your goal is to produce quilts reminiscent of your family's heritage, begin by gathering books on antique quilts. Fortunately, many quilted masterpieces remain in museums or photographs for us to study. These are wonderful examples of the perseverance of talented craftswomen for us to learn from and enjoy. Look at the colors, the patchwork, and the appliqué designs. Closely observe the texture created by the stitches that hold the layers together. Some quilting is utilitarian, really quite mundane. Others demonstrate the time and consideration spent planning elaborate choices.

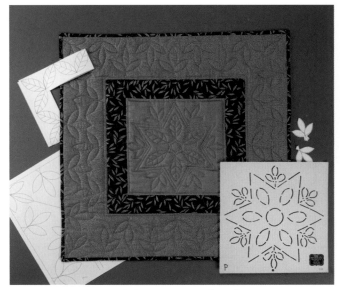

Simple shapes inspired the continuous-line designs.

Where did quilters from the past find the inspiration for their artwork? They utilized patterns found in nature, in architecture and in everyday objects that surrounded them. Patterns were repeated and altered through the years. Observe these simple shapes that were used within this pattern manufactured years ago for hand quilting. Look how it inspired my adaptations for continuous-line designs.

Where are you going to search first for inspiration? The ancient philosopher, Plato, suggests "Practice Wonder!" I was so impressed while learning about his life and his suggestion that we should approach life with a sense of wonder, not only to accept what we know, but to look for more. Be observant and ready to take action when you see designs that interest you. Keep your camera handy, or carry a sketchbook to record an idea. Add the results to your idea notebook.

As We Finish

What have you learned about choosing the perfect quilting design? The simple answer is to use what you like and what makes you happy. Now it's time to begin the process of filling quilt tops, knowing that you are unique and capable of making wonderful decisions. Who else could ever know what you think is perfect?

A gathering of a beautiful selection of fabrics, trims and adornments could inspire a theme for a quilt.

Lesson Two:

Sources For Design Images

Lesson Two will teach you how to broaden your
horizons when looking for inspiring designs.

Getting Started

Now that you have gathered great ideas for your project, you need to
know what to do if the desired designs are not available as quilting stencils.
With your heightened sense of awareness, you'll find that many designs you
can use for quilting have been staring you right in the face. Now you'll have
the information you need for putting them to use!

But even before you begin your search, take a moment to consider the
purpose for this quilt. You should begin any project by giving some thought
to the finished product, based on a realistic assessment of your ability and of
your time investment.

As you plan a quilt, ask yourself:

- Who will be the recipient of this quilt?

- Where and how will it be used?

- How sturdy does it need to be?

- How much time can I commit to this project?

- Is there a deadline for its completion?

- What techniques will be used for construction?

- What are my abilities for using these techniques?

Focus on the answers to these questions when setting criteria for making design decisions. Consider whether the quilt needs to be utilitarian, to withstand dorm life and frequent washings. You will choose different materials for this type of project than if you are making a decorative wall quilt. If the quilt is for a rough and tumble child, make it quickly using durable fabrics and let it be loved! If your project is to be a masterpiece given as a special gift, you may enjoy investing many hours on the details. The time you have to invest in the project will determine the scale and amount of quilting used.

Special quilted gifts don't always have to be bed quilts. Think about how this simple design, like the one in the photo, could be utilized for several quick projects like a wall quilt, a cover for a scrapbook or a pillow.

Exploring your ideas and translating your theme to a quilt.

Begin with a strong composition, just as you would when writing a paragraph or letter. The origin of your idea may have been burning within you before you began, or ignited because of an event you wish to commemorate. Follow these steps to adequately develop your idea, support it with details, and add your personal style.

1 Start with one topic and build on it. Make a list of words, images, shapes, feelings and events, anything that pops into your head that relates to your theme. Keep this list of ideas in view until the project is finished. One word or concept that may seem unimportant now could become a great inspiration later in the process.

2 Now visualize the theme and develop a list of pictures that express the idea. Add images such as:
- Baby—name, date, booties, hearts, duckies
- Sports—ball, shoes, team emblem, team colors
- Outdoorsman—fish, ducks, cattails, trees
- Music—instruments, notes, staff
- Sewing—spool, pincushion, needle, machine, scissors
- Wedding—bells, interlocking rings, double wedding ring pattern

3 Decide how you will convey the ideas. Will patchwork, appliqué or photos be used? Consider adding details with quilted images or letters to convey information. You can utilize the same skills to collect ideas for making quilting designs that are used when creating a scrapbook. Look at the memorabilia gathered from an event or trip to find inspiration for quilting designs.

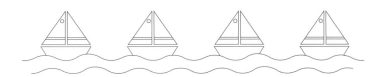

Where do I find new sources for quilting designs?

Now that you have ideas for stitching your quilt, it's time to find designs. If you don't have the ideal stencil or pattern from a quilting book, you'll need to search outside your regular sources:

- Dover Books offer a great source of copyright-free designs.

- Wrapping paper and greeting cards are a wonderful source of inspiration.*

- Surf the Internet for free clip art Web pages that offer unlimited ideas.*

- Study the books you own showing quilts, new and old, look at the quilting details.

- Go to the library and look for books on labels, pictographs and logos.

- Quilt design software has many images in the appliqué and quilting areas.

- Consider letting a fabric dictate the theme of your quilt. Look at your fabric stash and observe the designs. There could be characters or motifs that inspire your selections.*

*Respect copyright laws.
Know and respect copyright laws. Research whether antique designs or clip art are copyright-free materials. They often are. Never use someone else's designs for items you intend to sell without written permission. When exhibiting your quilts, give credit to any designer's work by including terms like "designs influenced by" or "my interpretation of the artist's work."

This group of ribbons, trim and silk was gathered on a trip to Paris. Won't it be fun to explore these motifs to use as quilting designs?

Let the fabric inspire the theme of the quilt.

Wouldn't it be a great idea to make a quilt to capture the memories of a wonderful trip or vacation? This quilt was made with a grapevine theme, reminiscent of a memorable trip to Napa Valley, the heart of California's wine industry. Postcards, labels from the wine bottles and vineyards logos all added to the inspiration of the piece.

Begin collecting fabrics that support the theme. For this quilt, a focus fabric with a grape print offered the color scheme and the other fabrics were chosen to complement it.

A patchwork grapevine wreath was created from a pattern of unusual blocks and arranged in a wreath shape.

Add quilting designs to the layout. Original illustrations of grape clusters fill the center, corners and borders of the quilt.

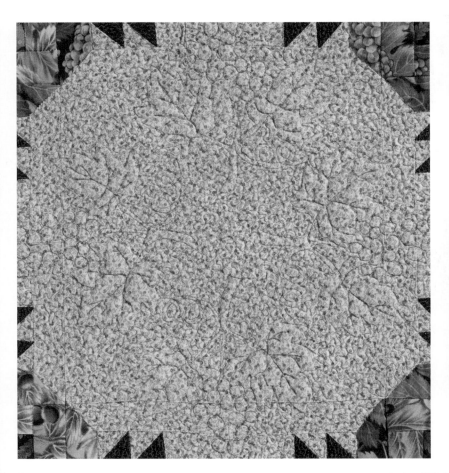

Bountiful Vineyard Quilt by the Author 2001

As We Finish

Take a moment to question your goal before you begin any project in life, not just quilting. Some projects don't warrant the time to look for extraordinary quilting designs, while other projects become special because of your efforts. When you understand your intentions and have appropriate images, move on to making templates and sizing the designs to fit your needs.

When you construct a project, implement your best craft skills to support your design efforts. Be realistic about your abilities, a simple pattern that is well executed is better than complicated patchwork with points that don't match. By choosing to read this book, you have demonstrated a desire to create quilts that are unique and personal. Make today the day you also become determined to set higher standards for your work . Expect more of yourself and practice until you achieve a higher skill level. And, for goodness sake, take time to celebrate your accomplishments!

Lesson Three:

Making Full-Size Templates

In the next three lessons, you will:

- Use paper to re-create each of the spaces of the quilt top that need to be filled.

- Learn interesting ways to divide those spaces.

- Adapt and resize designs to fill the spaces.

Just wait until you learn the logical process to solving the mystery of creating designs to fit!

Getting Started

Wouldn't it be sweet if the quilting stencils you have been collecting all these years actually fit your quilt tops exactly? And, since we are daydreaming, the block stencils you own would coordinate with border stencils in every size needed, and the borders have mitered corners that turn exactly in the right place for your quilt. Imagine how that would simplify your quilting life!

Consider how efficient the quilting process will be when you begin with a perfectly sized template for every empty space of your project, and then apply my simple instructions for filling those spaces with coordinating designs.

Working Full Size

Begin by applying this step-by-step process to the exercise project, or to any top that you might have waiting to be quilted.

The layout for our exercise project is very simple, and may be a bit elementary for your skill level. Remember, this is just a lesson and it's supposed to be easy. The layout provides three distinct areas to fill with coordinating designs and provides a versatile base for demonstrating the next several lessons. Follow the sizes given to construct a 30" pieced top from fabric, or learn by making the paper templates.

Supply Needs

Pencils and eraser
Paper, long rolls
Scissors to cut paper
Quilting stencil
Two rulers, any 6" to 12" square
and any 18" to 24" rectangle
with a 45° line

Fabric Needs

¾ yd. medium- to large-print
 fabric for the outer border as a
 focus fabric
¼ yd. small-print fabric
½ yd. medium- to light-colored
 solid or almost solid fabric
Thread in a coordinating color

Cut the Top

How Many	Fabric	Size	For
1	Solid	12½" x 12½"	Center square
2	Small print	12½" x 3½"	Narrow inner-border strips
2	Small print	18½" x 3½"	Narrow inner-border strips
2	Focus or border print	18½" x 6½"	Wide outer-border strips
2	Focus or border print	30" x 6½"	Wide outer-border strips

Assemble the Top

1 Assemble the top using ¼" seam allowances.

2 Sew one inner-border strip to each side of the center square, press seams open, then attach the top and bottom strips, then press.

3 Attach the wide outer-border strips in the same manner.

Do *not* layer with batting or backing before marking.

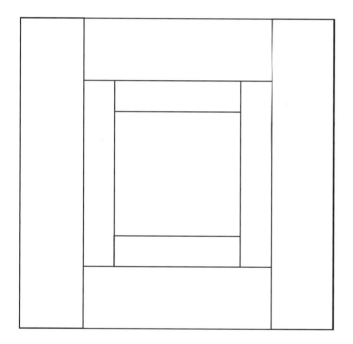

tip:
Begin any project by pressing the fabric using spray starch to stabilize it before cutting, as well as during the assembly process. This increases the accuracy of the pieced top. Pressing the seams open distributes the layers evenly for machine quilting.

Making Perfect Templates

Now you'll make paper templates for the spaces of the assembled top. Use any paper that is large enough, taping pieces together if necessary. Begin with one square and two strips for each size border. You can cut more later if needed.

- Measure the center block and cut a paper template that matches the finished size.

- Measure the width and length of the outside edge of the *long* narrow border. Cut two paper strips the exact size of the border. (For our exercise, 18" x 3".)

- Measure the width and length of the outside edge of the *long* wide border. Omit the space that will be covered with binding from this measurement. Cut two paper strips the exact size of the border. (For our exercise these are 30" x 6".)

How can I apply this lesson to other projects?

Now that you know how to make templates, you can follow this process for any project, even if it has already been pieced. Begin by neatly pressing the finished top. Measure the spaces and make the needed templates. Remember to measure the *longest* edge of each size border strip and omit the area that will be covered when the binding is added.

If the project has setting triangles, measure the distance from the right angle corner to the pointed corner. On a piece of paper, mark that distance from the corner along each side and then draw a line to connect the two marks. Any triangular spaces with varying degrees of angles are drawn in a similar manner.

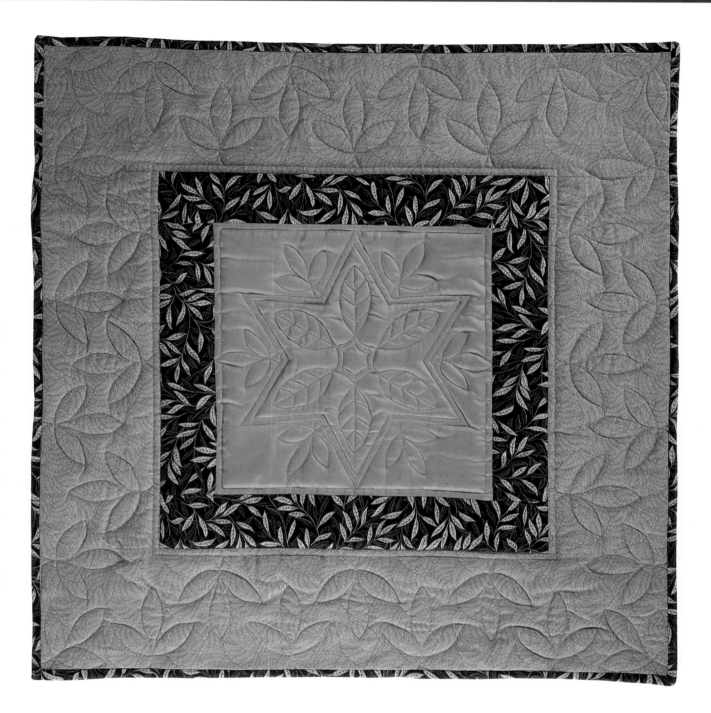

As We Finish

That is all it takes to get started making perfect-fitting templates! Can you see how this simple process will help you when creating other projects? Next, we'll consider the many ways in which the spaces can be divided and then how to resize your designs to fit. Let's get to it!

Lesson Four:

Exploring the Division of Space

Getting Started

Continue your exercise by looking at the many options for dividing the paper templates into segments that you'll fill with designs. Folding creases in the paper provides a quick and accurate method for indicating the segments and placement lines.

We will need several motifs (individual quilting designs) to play with. Trace several copies of any simple drawing or quilting stencil on paper and cut them out. Try one design that is symmetrical (having identical left and right halves) and one that is asymmetrical.

Don't worry about the size of the motifs. You are just auditioning the many ways to divide the templates into segments, which will help you understand what size is actually needed for the design.

It might be fun to hang your assembled quilt top on a design wall to audition possible choices as you work. Patterns can look very different from a vertical view versus a horizontal one. Stand back and let your creativity burst forth!

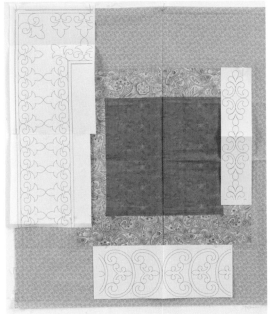

tip:
Keep creases precise by making the first crease, unfold the paper, folding the second crease, unfold, and continue for all necessary folds. Or if you prefer, use a ruler and pencil to measure and then draw lines indicating the segments.

Continuing Your Exercise

Begin by dividing the paper square. Fold a crease down the center and across the middle, dividing it into four smaller squares, referred to as quarters. Look at ways a motif could be placed using these divisions.

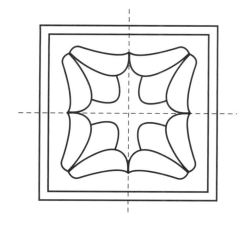

- Try facing the motifs toward the center of the block, edges touching.

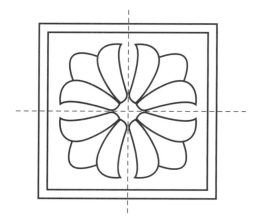

- Try turning them away from the center.

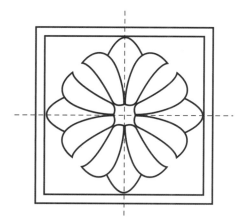

- Try centering a motif *on* the folds rather than *in* the sections.

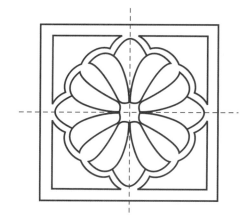

- Add a line ¼" away from the motifs to fill in the corners.

Isn't it interesting how the designs can look so different with such simple alterations? All those choices came from just two folds in the template. Let's try some different folds.

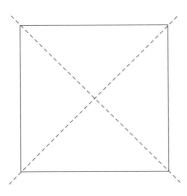

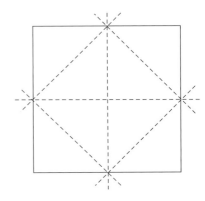

- What if you crease the square from corner to corner?

- Or fold the square in half and then half of that half, into 16 little squares?

- Or try folding the square in quarters and then on the diagonal across the quarters.

Have I gotten you thinking? Aren't you glad we have more paper? Now let's get to work on the borders. They can be divided in numerous ways and their intersections provide many mitering options.

Dividing the Narrow Borders

Now we can begin to explore options for filling the border templates. By dividing them into segments, we will determine the exact size needed for the individual motifs. Let's start looking at the possibilities for dividing the space before we consider filling it.

Divide the 3" x 18" template into equal segments and place a motif sized to fit in each segment.

Creating a Mitered Template

Fold the end of each strip at a 45-degree angle forming a mitered corner that starts nearest the center of the quilt and points to the outside edge.

Cut off the folded triangles on each side so that two strips fit together. Now the inner border length measures 12" toward the center of the quilt and 18" toward the outer border.

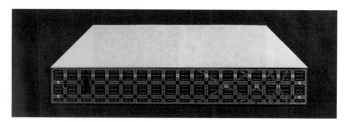

Notice how the motifs of one design cover two narrow border strips.

Did folding the corner throw you off? If we had only measured the outside edge of the border, and did not consider that the border strips would overlap at the corners, our templates would be too long. If we measured only the inside edge, our templates would be too short.

tip:

A simple solution for filling narrow borders is to use one quilting design to cover two or more border strips of fabric. Measure the combined spaces to make the template.

Determining the Perfect Segments

- Fold the strip in half, making a crease crosswise, indicating the center of the length of the template. This is the centerline.
- Draw a lengthwise line down the middle of the width of the template.
- Measure the length of the line.
- Measure the width of your motif.

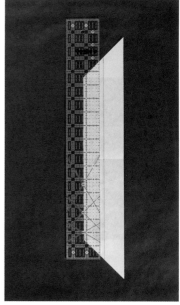

To determine the number of segments needed, divide the length of the line by the width of the motif. If the answer is not a whole number, you will have to resize your motif or use an alternate suggestion that we will discuss later.

Draw marks along the line that are the width of the motif to indicate where to fold the strip into segments. The length of the line of our exercise is 15". It can be divided into two 7½" segments, three 5" segments, four 3¾" segments and so on. In a perfect world, your motif is one of those measurements and ends at the point where the line meets the cut edge of the strip.

- Center a motif in each segment. Sometimes a motif may be a bit too large or too small. In Lesson Five we will learn how to measure the segment and alter the size of the motif on a copy machine.

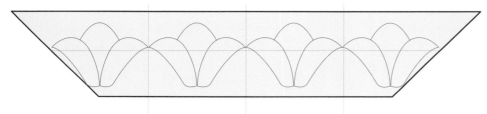

These motifs measure 3¾" and fit perfectly.

- Or, try centering the first motif on the centerline. Then fold the rest of the strip into segments that are the width of the motif.

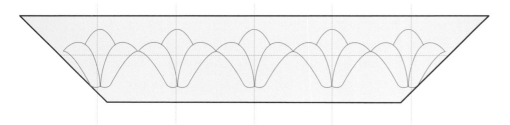

These motifs measure 3" and fit perfectly.

tip:
Use this process to determine the number of motifs needed when working on projects with long borders. Divide the length of the centerline by the size of your motifs. If the number is even, place the motif next to the centerfold. If the number is odd, center the motif on the centerfold.

Dividing the Wide Border

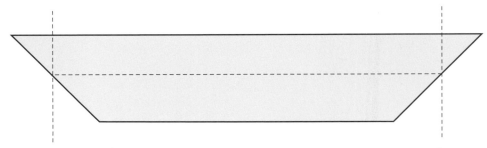

Follow the instructions for dividing the large border in the same manner as the narrow border, drawing the centerline in the middle of the strip, lengthwise. The measurement of the line is 24", yielding three 8" segments, four 6" segments, five 4⅘" segments, six 4" segments, and so on.

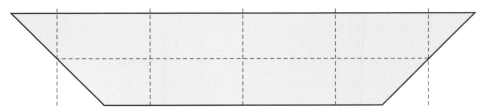

Does it seem that this demonstration goes against conventional thinking? If the border is 30" long, shouldn't it divide into five segments that are 6" long? It can be divided that way, so read on for examples of how to fill these spaces. When the corner space is shared for a mitered design, you must divide the length of the line. And, did you notice the end segments are a different shape than the others? We will learn about that in Lesson Five.

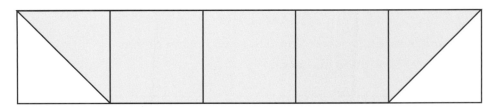

However, you must consider that when the corner spaces are shared for a mitered design, the end segments are a different shape than the other segments. In this case, the length of the centerline must be divided to determine the size of the motifs. You'll learn more about filling spaces in Lesson Five.

Adjusting the Space to Fit Your Motifs

Here is another concept to consider that may seem complicated at first, but let me explain. There may be times when this small adjustment to where the line is drawn will be all it takes to make a "slightly off" stencil fit the border just right.

By simply moving the line off center, we can change its length.

Changing the position of the line that the motifs are placed on, in relationship to the lengthwise middle of the border, will affect the length of the line. Consequently, the placement of the motifs on that line, in relationship to the distance from the center of the quilt, will affect the space that they fill. So, if your motifs don't quite fit the segments, simply move them above or below the lengthwise middle of the border, provided the space is wide enough for the motif to fit the width of the border.

For example, your motif is 4¼" long. Fold the 24" line into six 4" segments. Place the paper motif cutouts as far above the line, (farthest from the center of the quilt) as needed to fill each segment. Add several lines of stitching or a row of simple objects to fill in the extra space created by placing the motifs off center.

Keep this guide in mind when dividing long borders:

- If the border segments are slightly long for the width of the motif, move the row of motifs closer to the quilt center.

- Move the motifs farther from the quilt center if the border segments are too small.

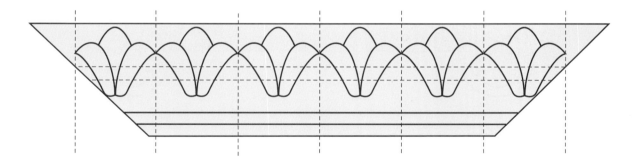

Adjust the stencil to fit a border by sliding it off center. Several lines of stitching fill in the extra space.

To Miter or Not to Miter, That Is the Question

Let's try some options for turning a mitered corner. You'll work with the paper motifs to determine your favorite choice. Begin with the wide border, since the extra width allows more ways to position the motif. You'll discover that the amount of space the motifs use to fill the corner will determine the number of segments needed to fill the rest of the border.

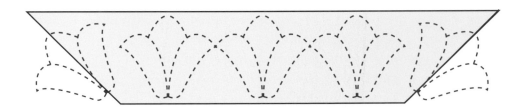

- Try centering the motif diagonally on the corner line.

- Try a mirror image. This motif fills the space nicely.

• Consider using another complete motif to fill the empty space.

• Consider using a portion of the motif to produce a coordinating design to fill the space.

Not happy with your results? Does it seem that no matter how you place the motifs, they just don't look right? Here are several ideas that do not require mitering the corners at all.

Using Corner Designs

Here is an idea that worked well for this layout. Place a pair of motifs *only* in the corners of the border and then use a grid or stippling to fill in the rest of the space.

OK, you caught me! They do actually form a mitered corner, but this was an attractive solution when the border segments didn't quite fit. An additional pair of motifs was used on the center line of the long border for this rectangular table runner.

Using Corner Blocks

There are instances when running the border design into a corner block may be a better choice than slicing a fussy design at an unpleasant angle. Just because you cut the templates at a 45° angle to produce the accurate template doesn't mean you always have to use the space in that manner.

Corner blocks are square designs made from portions of the motifs used in the project or a square design from another source that coordinates with your theme. If you are using a block stencil that is slightly larger than the width of the border, consider reducing its size and using it as a corner block. Stitching a double outline around the square will distinguish it from the border design.

When using corner blocks, make new templates from the original measurements, 18" x 3" for the narrow border and 30" x 6" for the wide border.

- For the narrow border, draw straight lines on one template where the inside edges of the border overlap, forming a 3" x 3" square for the corner block template. Cut the other template 12" x 3".

- For the wide border, draw straight lines on one template where the inside edges overlap, forming a 6" x 6" square corner block and an 18" x 6" border template.

A Bit of History

Years ago, many quiltmakers from didn't concern themselves with perfectly-mitered corners on their quilts. Many antique quilts have border motifs that just run into the side of the quilt and another motif begins at a right angle to the first border.

Apply the Lesson to Future Projects

Creating templates for any patchwork or appliqué project will be easy when you apply the measuring and dividing techniques you have just learned. Transfer these ideas to differently shaped spaces that you want to fill.

- Begin with a neatly pressed top.

- Make the template by laying a sheet of tracing paper over the pieced top and transfer the outlines of the spaces. This is easier than measuring a large piece.

- Lay tracing paper over a pieced block, outlining each space within the block. Use this template to plan the quilting lines needed to anchor the block and to evenly distribute quilting over the surface of the quilt. You might discover a very unique quilting design for plain blocks and setting triangles.

tip:

When working on the quilting plan for a patchwork quilt, use this simple suggestion for determining how many segments are needed and how large to make them. Consider using the size of the patchwork block as a guide to dictate motif size as well as the number of repeats. For example, if your top has ten rows of 6" blocks, fold the border template into ten segments and adjust the motif size to be 6" long. Or, use two motifs in each segment that measure 3" long, and so on.

As We Finish

I hope you enjoyed this simple exercise. Templates are so helpful, and now you can create them for any future project. In Lessons Five and Six, you'll learn how to fill spaces with coordinating designs.

Quilting design from **Claire** *Elements Stencil Packet.*

Lesson Five:

Adapting Designs to Fit Your Spaces

Getting Started

By now, you must be anxious to play with shapes and placement of images. Learning to adapt a motif frees you from using it only as the manufacturer expected. By merely changing the size, rotating its orientation, or selecting portions to be used on their own, you can manipulate any motif to fit your needs.

You may be satisfied to just follow along, filling spaces and moving right on to marking and quilting. Do that if you must, but there are many more ideas here and a lot more fun to be had by trying them!

tip:

A good sense of proportions keep a pleasing relationship between the scale of one design used throughout the layout by not increasing or decreasing it more than 20%. That is, a tiny motif may need to be increased several hundred percent to get it to a stitchable size, but once that size is established, don't make changes to it or to sections that are too drastically different within that project.

Changing a Motif Size With the Proportional Scale (on the first try!)

Use motifs traced onto paper from a manufactured stencil, or any stitchable design created from other sources.

- Measure the size of the quilting design. This is your "original size."

- Next, measure the space that needs to be filled. This is the "reproduction size."

- Locate the original size on the scale.

- Rotate the dial, matching the original to the reproduction size.

- Hold the dial securely as you check the calculated result in the window.

- The figure indicated by the arrow in the window is the number (percentage) to set the copy machine to enlarge or reduce the design.

Proportional scale and the same design in two different sizes.

Inverting the Direction of a Design With a Copy Machine

For this exercise, you'll need copies of an asymmetrical motif to play with that are printed out in mirror images of one another. First, check the copy machine for a mirror image task button. If it has one, use it. If not, carefully trace the outline of the design on tracing paper (or on lightweight white paper), flip the paper over, and copy it with a white sheet of paper covering the design. The result will be a mirror image of the original.

Flipping Motifs in the Border Segments

Discover many interesting and varied designs by turning the motifs in different directions. Keep your eye on how the corner spaces are filled.

- Placing motifs all facing the same direction works well for uneven numbers.

The motif is used side-by-side, parallel to the edge of the quilt.

- For an even number of motifs, direct half toward the left and half toward the right.

- Place motifs facing one another, forming pairs.

- Turn the design parallel to the quilt edge. Alternate the motifs facing the center of the quilt and touching the outside edge, filling the width of the border. The corner space is filled with a portion of the motif.

Freebie Square Designs

Do you see what I see? By working out attractive solutions for your mitered corners, wonderful bonus designs are created that fill half or one quarter of a square space. This is an example of using repetition of designs to your advantage within the layout.

Study how these square designs were created by joining the mitered corner solutions from the border.

Place the curved side of the motif to the outside of the design.

Turn the curved side of the motif toward the center.

Now try the same design on point.

Rotate the design on point.

Create a larger design with four pairs of the motif and look at the design on point.

Work with the motif pairs to create more options and rotate the design.

The center of the design is filled with another set of motifs that were slightly reduced to fit the empty space.

Look at these! Two new designs are created from a group of three motifs.

In some of the border examples, parts of the motif were used to fill empty corner spaces. Look at the beautiful design created by placing four mitered corners together.

Now flip those designs so that the corners meet in the center.

As We Finish

Repetition and rotation can offer amazing variety within the quilting layout. Print several copies of the motifs from the CD and let your creativity loose. In Lesson Six, you'll learn more techniques to fill the spaces of the quilt top.

Lesson Six:

Exercising Your Creativity

By tapping your creative potential, you'll add pizzazz that makes your quilts unique.

In this lesson, we'll explore more options for changing the motifs to fit our needs. You will:

- Divide the spaces in ways that are more complex
- Add personal touches to existing designs
- Learn how sections of a motif can stand alone to create new coordinating options

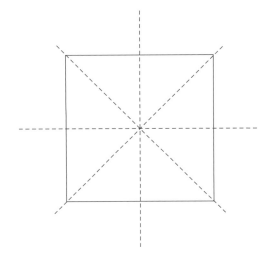

To use circular designs to fill a square space, divide the square into eight sections by folding it in half in each direction and then from corner to corner on both diagonals. Look how the shapes of the segments vary.

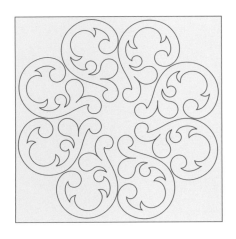

- Place one motif in each segment, radiating outward to form the wreath.

- Try alternating the motifs facing each other. Notice the wonderful design that is created in the center. Add a ¼" echo line as a corner detail to fill the space.

- Try rotating the pairs in the opposite direction and fill the center space.

Are you inspired to create designs to fill a wedge or pie-shaped space? Try creating some wedge-shaped designs from a motif. Or, fill the wedges with diamond-shaped designs that look like star points. The world of possibilities is open to you now that you have the foundation for making paper templates. This only takes a little paper and time, so have fun!

Adapting the Position of a Design to Fit Your Border

Many new and interesting designs can be created from a stencil if you position the motifs in a new direction. Play with the possibilities of tilting the motif at various angles, or try pairs of motifs to create new designs. When you are satisfied the best option has been found, add a small strip of tape indicating the degree of angle, so it can be easily repeated.

Selecting Designs as Secondary Motifs

Whether working with a simple motif or a complex design source, consider using portions of those motifs to yield several coordinating designs. Isolate one section of the design, trace it, or make some copies to work with.

- This narrow border was created by utilizing a portion of a simple motif.

- A new design is developed by using mirror images of the design.

- Make a new design by reflecting the single-row design to form a double-row border.

- If the selected area is small, try using it as a corner block.

tip:

When marking a partial design with a stencil, cover the unused portion with masking tape. Try repeating the section as a border in all of the various options you have learned.

Time and attention to detail contributed to the success of this piece. Portions of a larger acanthus leaf design were transformed into the small repeated motifs used for the border and corner blocks.

Filling the Border With Triangular Shapes

Cutting the ends of the border template on the diagonal provides an option for filling the border with triangular sections.

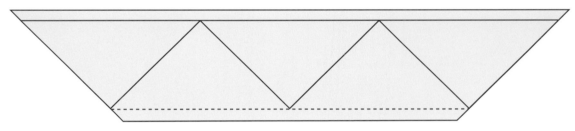

To determine the number of segments needed:
- Measure the length of the long side of the triangular template.
- Measure the length of the long edge of the border strip.
- Divide the border length by the size of the triangle.

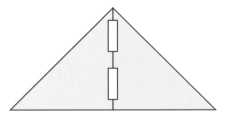

- Tape together the two ends you cut from the border template to make the triangular template.

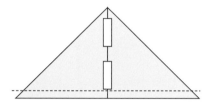 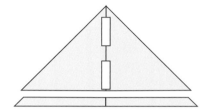

Adjustments to the triangle may be needed to fit the border space. If the border segment is shorter than the length of the template, trim the long edge of the triangle to match the width of the segment. Resize the motifs to fill the space.

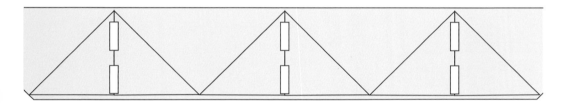

If the border segment is larger than the template, fill the template with the motif and add a row of stitching to outline the space.

Now, have fun manipulating design pairs to fill a triangular shape. In this example, the design has been rotated to fit the same degree of angle as the template. It is then re-sized to fill half of the template and copied to produce the mirror image. To completely fill the space, a line was added ¼" from the designs and the edge of the template.

Bonus Square!

How well are you trained to visualize new designs? By using a pair of the triangular border motifs on point, a square layout is created. Notice how additional lines extend the size of the design to fill a larger space.

Add Personal Details to Your Own Design Style

Learning free-motion quilting increases your ability to stitch complex designs quickly and easily. It sparks your interest to find more advanced designs to stitch. Look at what exciting things can happen when you add your unique flair to an ordinary design. Try these ideas to embellish a simple stencil or design while keeping the principles of proportion in mind.

- Combine portions of several stencils to create new designs.
- Divide sections within the design by adding lines.
- Add fillers like grids, outlines and echo quilting.

Adding Text to Your Designs

Using alphabet letters created from your computer and printer is a great source for quilting designs. Many fonts are easy to stitch if they are large enough. Print out the selected words as large as the printer allows and enlarge as needed on a copy machine.

Many commemorative quilts are enhanced by adding information like initials, emblems and names to the quilting layout.

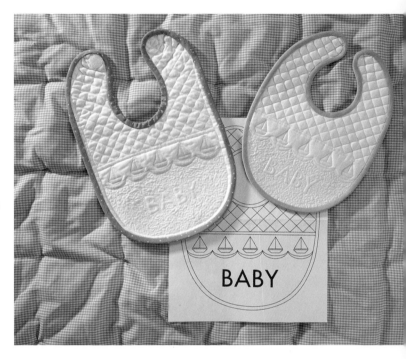

The completion date for this quilt was printed from a computer and used as a quilting design.

As We Finish

I hope your head is filled with ideas to alter the designs you own into new creations! Have you put down this book to dig out an old stencil that you now know will provide many new designs? And you didn't think you were artistic!

Expanding the use of one theme to fill all areas throughout the quilt reinforces one of the most useful design elements, which is repetition. Having the knowledge of how to implement this simple process will ignite a desire within you to create your own unique designs and never settle for the "expected" ever again.

This combination design is available as an **Options** *interchangeable stencil called* **Georgia** *produced by Golden Threads.*

Lesson Seven:

What You Have and What You Need

Getting Started

In this lesson, you'll discover how to use your stencils and the designs on the enclosed CD to create multi-sized borders from blocks. You'll find beautiful blocks hiding in your border stencils. We are going to play the "what if?" game. Won't it be fun, using what you already own to make something new? Follow the instructions to extend the use of designs for the greater purpose of filling blocks, setting triangles and multi-sized borders with coordinating designs.

I have included a large, complex block design on the CD to provide you with interesting examples. By using small sections of the designs you will find many solutions for the "What ifs?"

What if I have a block stencil, but it is the wrong size?

Let's begin with something simple, such as adjusting the size of a block stencil to fit the needed space. The simplest change would be to trace the design onto paper and change the size on a copy machine. But, you paid good money to use the stencil to make marking easier, so let's try some other ideas to make marking easier..

- Add a line of stitching, outlining the entire stencil.

- Add a portion of the design to fill the corners.

- Turn the stencil on point and add a square outline.

- Add a row of stitching that echoes the outline of each motif.

- Move the motifs away from the center of the square and add a simple object in between each motif.

What if my block stencil design is a tiny bit off?

In Lesson Five you learned how to adjust the placement of the motifs in relationship to the distance from the quilt center to fit the border. The same principle applies to squares and setting triangles. Moving motifs closer to the center of the square makes the group smaller, moving them out spreads the design and increases the space filled.

What if my block stencil design is too big for the space I have created?

- Isolate one section of the design and create new squares by placing the motif in one of the block layout options from Lesson Five.

- Isolate one motif and spin into a wreath design.

- Try a different portion of the design.

- Alternate motifs toward the center of the block and outward in a wreath.

What if I only have a border stencil and my quilt has blocks to fill?

One motif was manipulated to create all these different square layouts.

What if I only have a block stencil and I need varying size borders?

Trace the main motif, make several copies, and:

- Repeat the motif in rows as a border using one of the layouts suggested in Lesson Five.

- Rotate the design and position all in one direction.

- Alternate the motifs, one up and one down.

- Place double rows of motifs to fill a wide space.

What if my border design is the right length, but I have too much empty space surrounding it?

- Combine two border designs to fill the space.

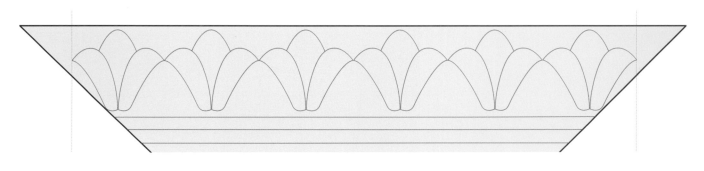

- Add lines of stitching to fill the space.

What if the motif is too small for a border segment?

- Center the motif in the segment of your template and leave a bit of space between each design. Remember, stippling can be used as a means of traveling from one motif to another, if it's being used as a background filler.

- Stretch the pattern slightly as you are marking, but don't distort the nice pattern.

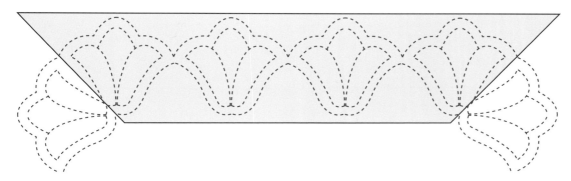

- Center a motif in each segment and add an outline around the motif.

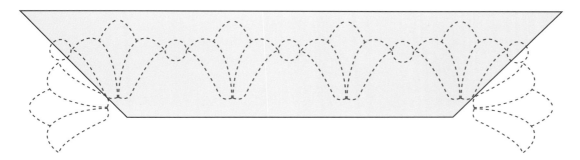

- Add a filler object in between each motif to fill in space.

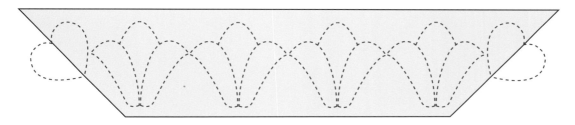

- Add a filler object to the end of the row as needed to fill the space evenly.

What if I only have a block design and I need setting triangles?

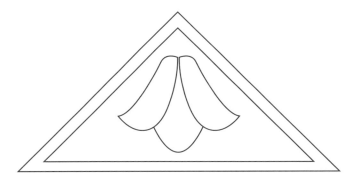

- Try placing an isolated motif on the diagonal of the triangle with its broadest part in the widest part of the triangle.

- Cut the design across the middle on the diagonal, using half of the design.

- Cut the design across the middle, placing the original design centers to the outside.

As We Finish

You have just absorbed a lot of practical information. Do you feel empowered to use that stack of stencils you have accumulated? I hope you found the illustrations helpful and you try new combinations of designs.

To Mark or Not to Mark

Getting Started

Now you are loaded with great designs that are the exact size you need, but some are stencils and some are printed on paper. You need to learn how to transfer the designs onto your fabric.

There are so many options for marking, or even not to mark at all. The fabric you are using will determine which method will work best. Fabrics that are dark colored, have busy printed designs, or cannot be washed, can pose a challenge. When I teach this class, students are always impressed with how many methods I have invented for marking intricate designs on difficult-to-mark fabric. Read all of the options to determine which is best for your project and refer back to the list for the best method for future projects.

You may think of marking as a tedious task. Would you feel better about the time spent on marking if you knew you were performing a valuable training exercise? An added bonus is that tracing the designs numerous times helps you to navigate the design when you are stitching!

I know that when I draw my own designs from scratch I can easily illustrate them with a sewing machine because my brain has already figured out how the parts connect. If you draw it, you can stitch it. Imprint the design into your brain by tracing, then you'll have the path to follow as you stitch.

Centering Your Design on the Fabric

Folding creases in the fabric is a quick and accurate way to determine the center of your fabric. Make a fold down the center and then across the middle, or on the diagonal. Match the fabric creases to the center of the paper design.

Marking Directly on Fabric

Many designs I use are original, drawn on a computer and printed onto paper. If the lines can be seen through the fabric, they can be traced with an inexpensive blue wash-away marker. A light box will help you see the printed lines through the fabric. The marker shows up surprisingly well on most fabrics. It can also be used when using stencils. To remove markings, submerge the entire piece in cold water until the lines are completely gone. Remove the piece from the water, and lay it flat to dry. If the marker reappears, you haven't gotten it all out. Repeat the removal instructions.

Follow this process if a light box is necessary to transfer designs printed on paper to dark fabrics. Tape the paper design to the lighted surface. Carefully center the fabric over the paper design and tape it down to avoid slipping.

Carefully trace the design with a white wash-away pen or pencil.

Whatever tool you choose, use a light touch. The less you put on, the less you have to take off. Before using any marking system, test it on swatches of the project fabric.

Additional Marking Tips:

- Never iron any fabric that has been marked; this could permanently set the markings in the fabric.
- Purchase several wash-away markers at a time. They dry out quickly and you don't want to run back to the store while working on a project.
- Masking tape is a great inexpensive marking aid for straight lines. Tape purchased at a painting supply store is less sticky and easier to remove.

Tracing Around the Outline of Objects

- If your motif is printed on paper, cut it out and trace around it, flip and rotate for added interest.
- Motifs can be cut out of freezer paper and temporarily fused to fabric.
- The same motifs cut from heat-resistant template plastic used for appliqué, can be used for marking quilting lines.

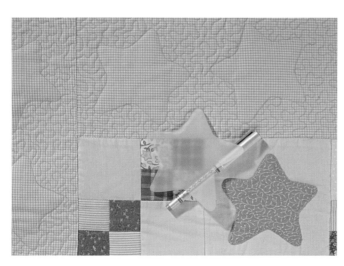

Making Your Own Stencil From Paper

Begin with a design that has been drawn on paper with a permanent marker or printed from your computer at the size needed. You will need several copies of the design if there are details within the design.

- Cover the paper with wide clear tape.
- Use a scissors to cut out the motif, leaving enough paper intact so the stencil does not fall apart.
- Cut slits in one of the other motifs indicating where to mark the detail.

Trace and Stitch Marking Methods

Trace the design onto Golden Threads Quilting Paper with any quilting pencil or marker. Pin the paper to the quilt surface and stitch through it. Gently pull the paper away from the stitches using caution not to pull on the stitches. Remove all of the paper fragments before any background quilting is stitched.

You can trace an entire border at one time and then stitch through the quilting paper. Measure the border strips as indicated in Lesson Four. Cut a template from the quilting paper for each border and fold it into the needed segments. Draw the motif on the top segment. Stitch through the folded paper without any thread in a sewing machine and when you unfold it, you have the design marked for the entire border.

You can mark a stack of blocks the same manner. Cut the paper the size of your fabric block plus 1" on all sides. Trace the design on the top piece of paper and stitch the design without thread. This method saves time if your stitching is accurate.

Quilting the Fabric Just as it is Printed

An added bonus of choosing an interesting focus fabric is that you may not need to mark over a busy design. Try using invisible thread and stitch, following the lines and curves of the fabric's printed design. I refer to fabrics with busy designs as "stitchable".

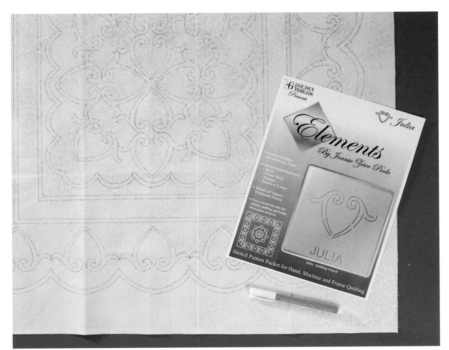

*Just a few scallops and double lines along with my **Julia** Stencil Packet were all it took to create this wholecloth layout.*

As We Finish

There are many additional tools and methods that are available for marking fabric. I have just provided a few that work for me. Experiment with these and others to find what you like best. Send me your innovative ideas!

Simple Clutch Purse
Finished Size: 9½" x 7"

When you realize how easy this little project is to construct, and how little time it takes to stitch, you'll want one for yourself and several as gifts for girl-friends. Consider how wonderful these bags would be for coordinating with bridesmaids' gowns or for a mother of the bride or groom. This is a very simple solution for keeping your necessities organized. And, this handmade purse would provide a wonderful remembrance of a special day.

Begin with a shopping trip to a specialty shop (or maybe your very own specialty stash) for some fancy fabrics. Choose a beautiful piece of silk or brocade and a complementary solid satin or sateen. Audition several lovely trims you have been saving. This project is adaptable to as many embellishments as you choose to use. What a great excuse to have some goodies on hand!

Materials

Fabric

½ yd. fancy fabric such as silk or brocade

½ yd. solid-colored fabric such as taffeta, sateen or satin

Notions

Batting

Quilt marking pen or pencil

Magnetic Clasp or VELCRO® closure

Ruler

½ yd. of ½" wide trim (optional)

Golden Threads Quilting Paper (optional)

Sewing machine with darning foot and (optional) walking foot

Cut the Materials

How Many	Fabric	Size	For
1	Fancy	11" x 16"	Center pattern
1	Solid	11" x 22"	Purse lining
2	Solid	10" x 14"	Quilted front flap
1	Batting	10" x 14"	Front flap
1	Batting	11" x 22"	Purse body

Throughout this book, you have learned how to adjust the size of a design to fit your needs. If this purse is not the perfect size for you, enlarge or reduce the design and cutting sizes to work best for your needs.

Design Prep

The purse's front panel is stitched and quilted as a separate panel, then stitched to the fancy fabric.

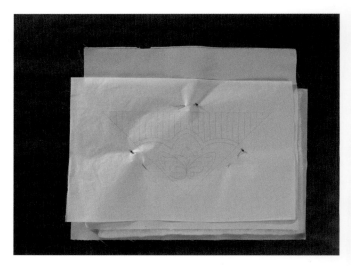

1 Copy the quilting design onto a sheet of quilting paper with a quilt marking pen or pencil. Use a ruler as a guide to keep lines straight.

2 Layer the lining, batting, and solid fabric with the pattern on top. Pin through all layers, avoiding the stitching lines.

- Begin quilting at the right side of the small circle of the leaf on the left. Bring the bobbin thread to the top. Hold the threads out of the way, stitch four or five locking stitches closely together, and travel to the bottom of the small circle. Stop with the needle down, clip the thread tails. Continue around the circle, crossing the starting point. Now, follow the scalloped line up to the top and then down toward the center of the design. As you pass the leaf veins, stitch up and retrace back on the same line to complete them. Continue to the bottom of the leaf outline, onto the top and complete the first leaf right where it meets the bud.

- Continuing with the same thread, stitch the lines within the bud. Stitch the scalloped line forming the bud over to the left leaf, retrace the same line back to the bud dome. Stitch it, retrace back to the right leaf.

- Stitch the right leaf in the same manner as the left, only in reverse. Secure the thread at the same place you began stitching on the first leaf.

- Begin a new thread at either side of the triangle near the double-arched line. Stitch across the design on the bottom line to the triangle outline on the other side, and back across the design on the other line.

- With the same thread, stitch around the entire outline of the triangle.

- Continue stitching the fill-in pattern with any line that is the closest to your stitching and follow it up to the top. Travel along the triangular outline to the next line, stitch back to the bouncing line, follow it over to the next line, back up and so on.

- You will need to begin one more thread to complete the fill pattern lines. Secure it on the triangle outline and finish the remaining lines. It took longer to write these instructions than it will take you to stitch it, but if you don't know where to travel, how will you get where you need to go?

3 Remove all of the quilting paper or the marker lines.

Assemble the Front Panel

1 If desired, sew trim along the edges of the quilted triangle before sewing the quilted panel to the fancy fabric.

2 Before trimming the triangle, place the fancy fabric piece and the quilted panel with right sides together. Using a walking foot, and with the quilted panel on the top, stitch a parallel line ⅜" from the quilting on the panel.

3 Flip the quilted panel back from the fancy fabric as shown. Trim all the layers.

Assemble the Purse

1 Layer the batting, lining and quilted panel together with the wrong side of the quilted panel facing up.

2 Sew around the entire edge of the purse leaving a 5" opening on the side for turning.

3 Turn the purse right-side out. Check all of your stitched seams.

4 Attach the magnetic closure, if desired.

5 Turn the purse wrong-side out and trim the corners and points.

6 Turn the purse right-side out and use a small crochet hook, or other pointed object, to gently square the corners.

7 Handstitch the opening closed.

8 Turn the bag wrong-side out and fold the bottom edge up and the top flap down, so the magnetic closure meets.

9 Pin side seams and then sew the seams. Secure the ends with extra tacking using handstitches.

10 Turn the bag right-side out and it is complete!

PUTTING IT ALL TOGETHER

I want to conclude this book by sharing this quilt I made in 2000, at the very beginning of my journey, back when this magic began happening in my life. This is the first piece I completed using the skill of heirloom machine quilting. I titled it 'Ode to Diane,' to honor my relationship with my teacher, Diane Gaudynski. The success I gained by taking her classes and learning this new skill has empowered me to believe in my aspirations — that building a career using art and quilting could be a reality.

All of the design skills used in creating this quilt are included in the lessons described for you in this book. The layout gave me an opportunity to create an elaborate original motif and then repeat segments of it to fill the many varied spaces of the top, thus creating unity. Paper templates were used to determine the sizes needed to fill the triangles, borders, and patchwork baskets.

The narrow quilted row of stitching on the saw-tooth border was a technique I copied from a similar quilt by Diane. Notice how I committed to having the entire surface of the piece covered with quilting that is evenly distributed and less than ¼" apart.

When you look at the quilts I am currently making and see how I have forged my own path to accomplish many unique designs, it may surprise you to know that I am not usually a very adventurous person in many areas of my everyday life. I'd rather have somebody else (OK, thank you Aaron) program my cell phone and just show me how it works than have to read its entire instruction manual. I could care less that I can't download 457 different ring tones for it from the Internet. I have no desire to travel into outer space or eat raw fish.

But, with my quilting, I am always striving for more; to try something unique that no one else has ever stitched before. That desire to expect more of myself has provided me with satisfaction for many achievements during this phase of my life.

The construction of a quilt can be a lot of work and a major investment of your time and money. Take my advice, the satisfaction of completing something challenging is so much greater than just going through the motions of staying at the same level you're at right now. Exciting things can happen if you work hard to make a design your own.

Use this book as a guide to help you. With it comes my wish that because you have this foundation of support, you will acquire the confidence to become adventurous in your quilting life. Ask yourself, what is the risk in learning something new and in expecting more of yourself, compared to the possible rewards? This is just some paper and a bit of fabric. (And I am guessing there is plenty more in your stash.)

I sincerely hope this journey into my workshop has enriched your quilting life. You now have the tools needed to work independently. I encourage you to explore new ideas. With each new project, turn the process into an expedition; travel to new heights with your quilting. Embark on your own independent adventure.

Joanie's
Design Elements
Gallery

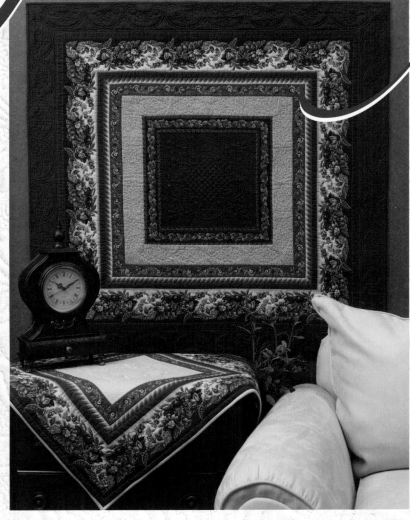

Camilla, *2005, printable quilting design found on CD.*

Ivy Wreath, *2004, original pattern for my Heirloom Machine Quilting class.*

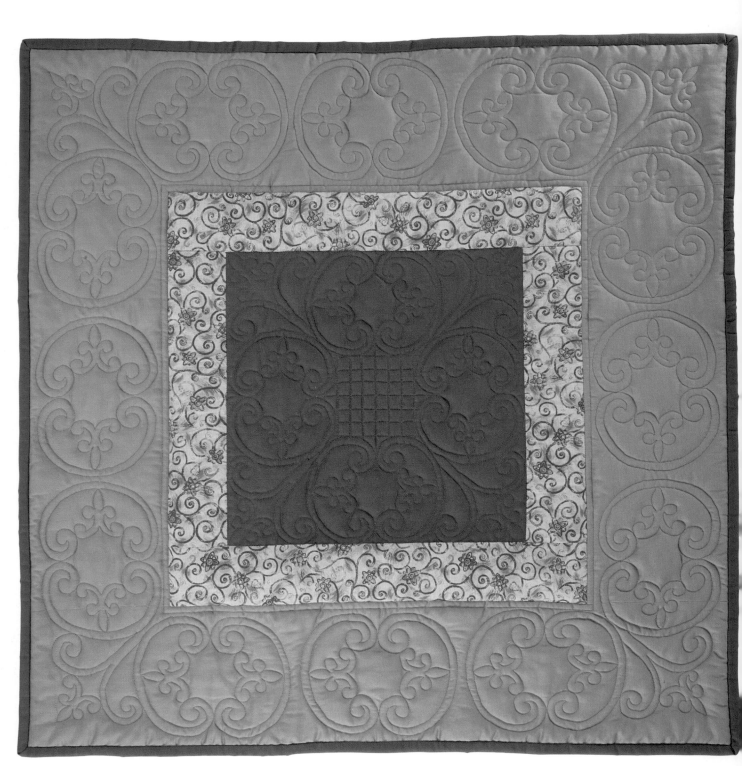

Camilla *alternate design, 2006, quilt layout on page 37 and printable designs on CD.*

Wholecloth featuring the Emma *Element Stencil Packet design.*

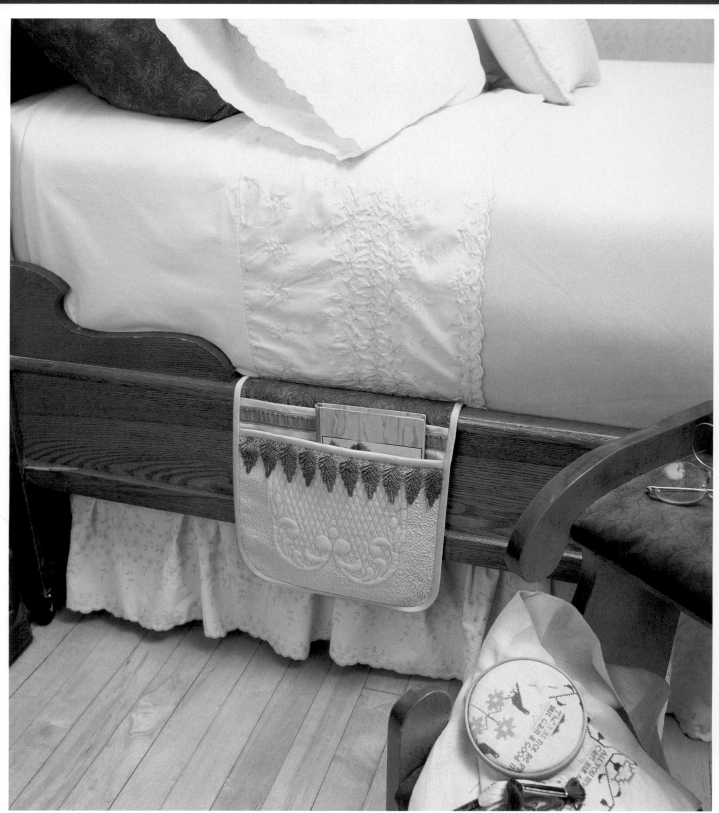

Bed tote pattern included in Elegant Machine Quilting.

This small quilt utilizes the Julia *Element Stencil Packet design.*

Autumn Leaves Table Runner pattern found in Elegant Machine Quilting.

Rich Holiday fabrics enhance the Claire *Element Stencil Packet design.*

Several designs from Elegant Machine Quilting *blend to create this wholecloth layout.*

Jewel, *2000, original design by the author.*

Classic Tiles Framed Corner Blocks pattern found in Elegant Machine Quilting.

Eggplant sateen jacket, placket embellished with Isabel *Element Stencil Packet design.* Simplicity *pattern 7100, www.simplicity.com*

Bountiful Vineyard, *2001, original designs by the author.*

Continuous line design inspired by a hand-quilting stencil.

Author's initial adorns this satin tie.

Camilla *alternate design, quilt layout on page 37 and printable quilting design found on CD.*

The author added her signature "checkerboard" pattern on the back panel of this Swing Jacket by Country in the City.
www.countryinthecity.net

Lantern Girls, *2006, quilt layout on page 37.*

Ode to Diane, *2000, by the author.*

SPONSORS

I would like to express my gratitude to the corporate sponsors for their generous support.

Elements Stencil Packets, designed by Joanie Poole
Options Interchangeable Stencils, designed by Joanie Poole

Golden Threads Quilting Paper
Golden Threads Proportion Scale
www.goldenthreads.com

Clover Marking Notions
www.clover-usa.com

Hobb's Wool Batting
www.hobbsbondedfibers.com

Piping Hot Binding Tool, by Susan Cleveland
www.PiecesBeWithYou.com

RJR Fabrics
www.rjrfabrics.com

Robert Kaufman Fabrics
www.robertkaufman.com

Superior Threads
www.superiorthreads.com

Supreme Slider
LaPierre Studios
www.freemotionslider.com

YLI Thread Corp.
www.ylicorp.com

This tiny piping is made with the aide of the Piping Hot Binding tool.

RESOURCES

Sewing Machines

Husqvarna/Viking
www.husqvarnaviking.com

Bernina
www.berninausa.com

Baby Lock
www.babylock.com

Singer
www.singerco.com

Janome
ww.janome.com

Pfaff
www.pfaff.com

Brother International Corp.
www.brothersews.com

Threads

YLI Thread Corp.
www.ylicorp.com

Coats & Clark
www.coatsandclark.com

Madeira
www.madeirausa.com

American & Efrid
www.amefird.com

Sulky of America
www.sulky.com

Supplies

Nancy's Notions
www.nancynotions.com

Keepsake Quilting
www.keepsakequilting.com

Connecting Threads
www.connectingtheads.com

Quilters Resource
www.quiltersresource.com

Books

Krause Publications
800.258.0929
www.krausebooks.com

Products

All artwork in this book is original and quilted on a domestic sewing machine by the author. Many designs used for the projects are located on the CD. Additional designs are available as *Elements* Stencil Packets and *Options* Interchangeable Stencils from Golden Threads, 888-477-7718 or www.goldenthreads.com

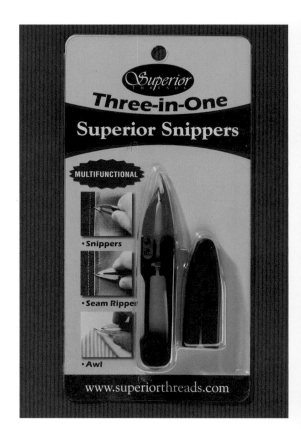

On The CD

4-1, 7 inch

4-2, 7 inch

4-3, 7 inch

4-4, 7 inch

4-4a, 7 inch

4-9, 2 inch

4-9, 3 inch

4-9, 4 inch

5-5a, 7 inch

5-5b, 7 inch

5-5c, 7 inch

5-5d, 7 inch

5-1, 5 inch

7-6, 10 inch

7-7a, 7 inch

Purse Design

5-2, 5 inch

7-7c, 7 inch

7-7b, 7 inch

7-10, 7 inch

7-7d, 7 inch

5-3, 5 inch

5-4, 4 inch

label?

7-12, 3 inch

7-13, 3 inch

7-14, 3 inch

7-15, 6 inch

About The Author

Author, pattern designer and award-winning quilt maker Joanie Zeier Poole has been a quilter all of her adult life and a practitioner of heirloom machine quilting on a domestic sewing machine for more than seven years. She fell in love with the art when she realized it would enable her to create the intricately embellished quilts of her dreams. Joanie started as a student of master quilter Diane Gaudynski, but she since has taken her craft to a level where she now teaches alongside her mentors and other top instructors at the Harriet Hargrave Machine Quilting Celebration.

Joanie uses this technique, along with her innovative appliqué and thread illustrations, to create original designs expressing her personal stories. Her quilts have been exhibited at major quilt shows and provoked an emotional connection with viewers. She received Best of Show honors at both Road to California 2006 and Pacific International Quilt Festival 2006.

A recent graphic design graduate, Joanie has chosen to blend her lifelong passion for quilt making with 21st century technology to create original patterns for quilting, appliqué and embroidery. Her first book, Elegant Machine Quilting, introduced readers to her innovative techniques and elegant style. She also uses her unique designs for her own pattern line and quilting products for Golden Threads.

For more about Joanie and her quilts, visit her Web site at www.heirloomquiltingdesigns.com.

Also Available From Krause Publications

Elegant Machine Quilting
Innovative Heirloom Quilting Using Any Sewing Machine
This 144-page book provides full-size templates for designs and incorporates the techniques into 20 simple projects, including table runners, napkins, wall hangings, a book cover, pillows and coasters. Order online at www.heirloomquiltingdesigns.com or www.krausebooks.com.
ISBN 13: 978-0-89349-878-4 • ISBN 10: 0-87349-898-4
$24.99 U.S.
#ELMQ

More Inspiration and Incentive for Expanding Your Skills

Elegant Machine Quilting
Innovative Heirloom Quilting using Any Sewing Machine
by Joanie Zeier Poole

Heirloom machine quilting can be done on a standard sewing machine, and Joanie shows you how in this one-of-a-kind quilting book! Detailed directions and thorough and colorful illustrations help you learn the basics of heirloom quilting, and take your machine quilting know-how to a new level, and into a new realm of possibilities.

In addition to providing general advice about choosing fabrics and making designs your own, you'll discover helpful color photos accompany tips on alternating patterns, selecting sizes, and more. Plus, the 20 featured heirloom projects include napkins, table runners, wall hangings and coasters.

Softcover • 8¼ x 10⅞ • 144 pages
200 color photos and illus.
Item# ELMQ • $24.99

The Quilter's Edge
Borders, Bindings and Finishing Touches
by Darlene Zimmerman

Bring a fabulous finish to any quilt with more than 200 step-by-step instructional color photos covering techniques including scalloped edges, curved edges, notched edges and more.

Softcover • 8¼ x 10⅞ • 128 pages
200+ color photos and illus.
Item# QLFT • $22.99

Designing Patchwork on Your Computer
by Carol Phillipson

This book/CD combo provides you with step-by-step instructions for designing a wide range of patchwork blocks, using just a few keystrokes.

Softcover • 8¼ x 9¼ • 128 pages
400 color photos and illus.
Item# Z0755 • $29.99
Bonus CD-ROM Included

Quilt As Desired
Your Guide to Straight-Line and Free-Motion Quilting
by Charlene C. Frable

Take your quilting skills to new heights with the six projects, using straight-line and free-motion techniques, featured in this revolutionary new guide. Discover what it means to truly quilt as desired.

Hardcover • 8¼ x 10⅞ • 128 pages
150 color photos
Item# Z0743 • $24.99

Contemporary Machine Embroidered Quilts
Innovative Techniques and Designs
by Eileen Roche

Moves from the basics of material selection and design, to twelve fabulous projects that combine quilting and embroidery. Patterns for quilts and embroidery designs are included on a free CD.

Softcover • 8¼ x 10⅞ • 144 pages
75 color photos, 75 illus., plus CD inserted
Item# MEQ • $27.99
Bonus CD-ROM Included